DEAR FRIENDS

This book will show you easy and fun it is to how to draw (pokemon) characteres

What you need : a pencil,an encar ,and color pencil

let's go......................

PEKATCHO

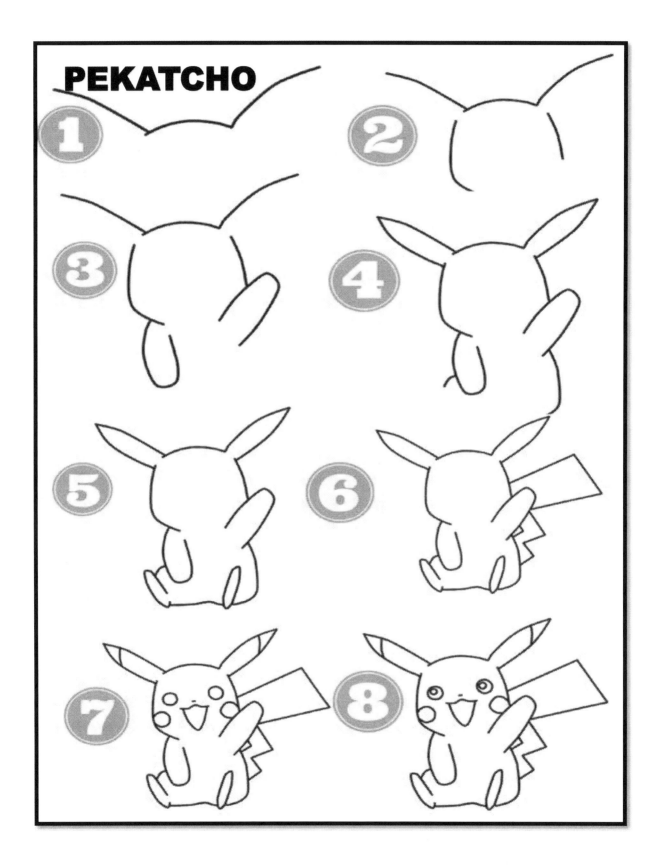

JIGGLIBAF

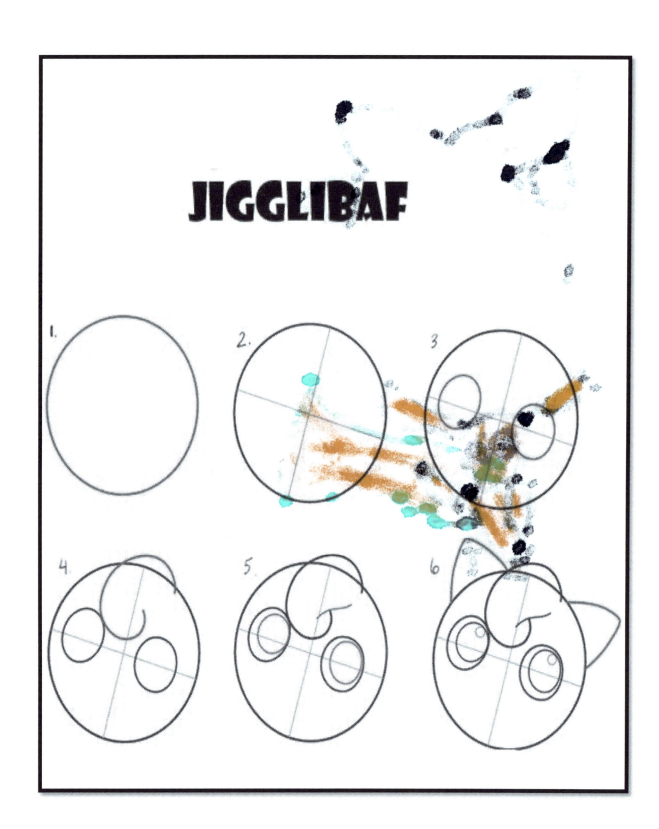

CUTE LEAFEON

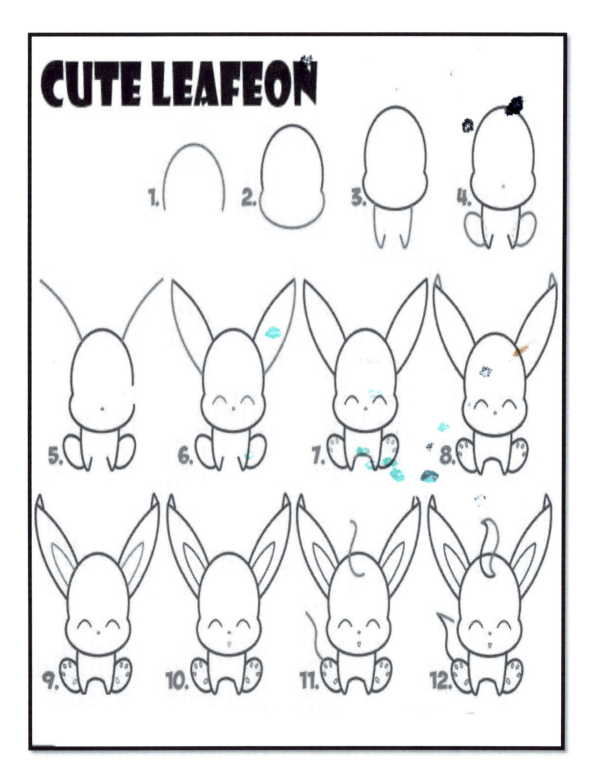

BUBLASAUR

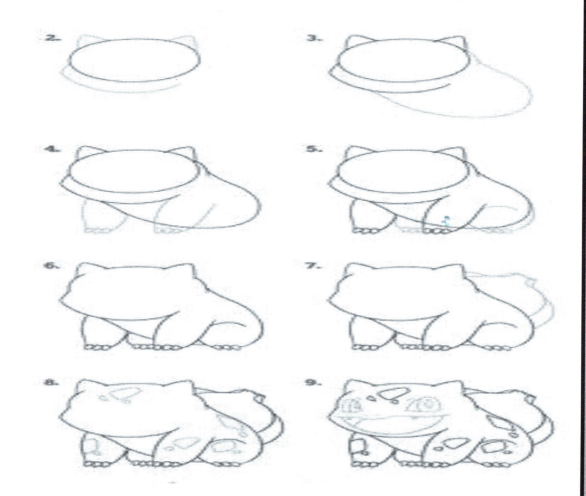

Charmander

2.

3.

4.

5.

6.

7.

8.

9.

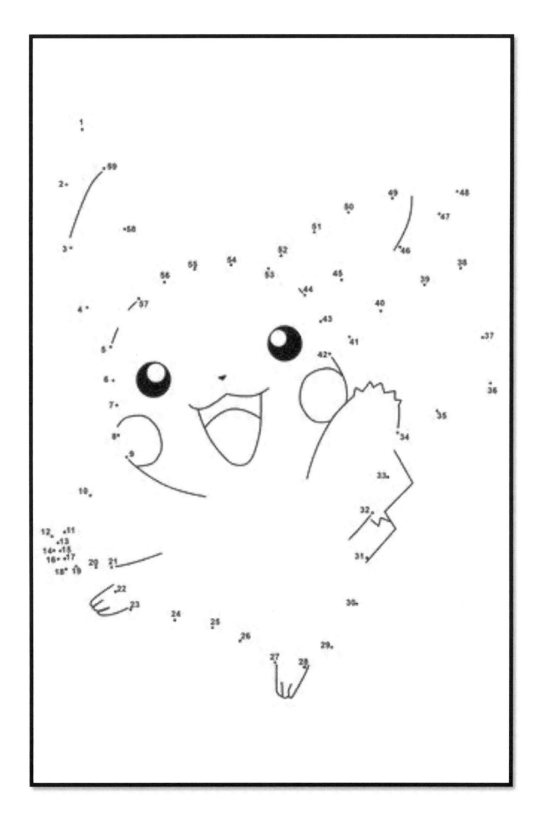

Squirtle

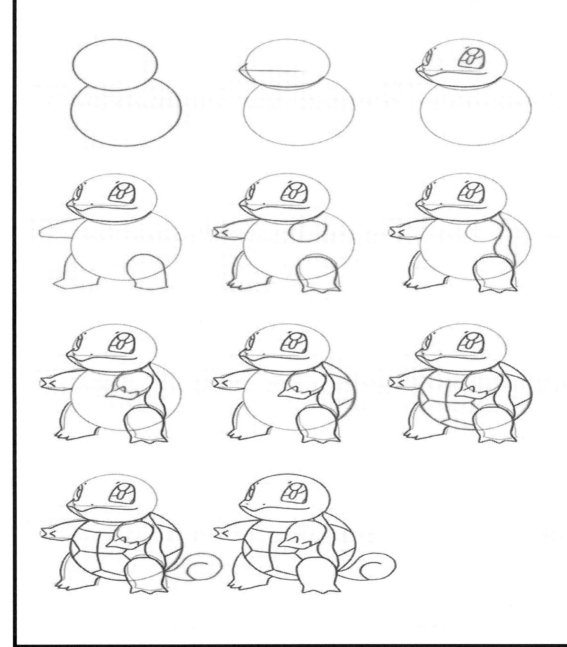

Pokeball

1.

2.

3.

4.

5.

6.

7.

8.

9.

10.

11.

Penguin

1.

2.

3.

4.

5.

6.

7.

8.

9.

Snorlax

EEVEE

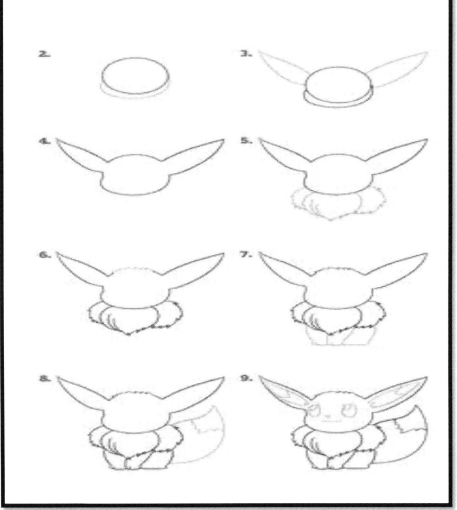

Ash ketchum

Gengar

2.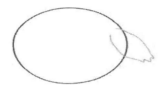

3.

4.

5.

6.

7.

8.

9.

Ash ketchum

Sandshrew

Manufactured by Amazon.ca
Bolton, ON

21403448R00020